Contents

© Copyright 1996 by Barron's Educational Series, Inc.
© Copyright 1995 by Gräfe and Unzer, GmbH, Munich, Germany.
The title of the German book is *Sterne*.

Translated from the German by Rita and Robert Kimber. Adapted and updated by Clint Hatchett, Director of the Science and Space Theater, Pensacola, Florida.

Photo credits: Work Collective Astrofotographie: front cover, pages 2–3, 13; Dresen: page 7 (top); NASA: page 9; Hamburg Planetarium: page 7 (bottom).

All inquiries should be addressed to:
Barron's Educational Series, Inc.
250 Wireless Boulevard, Hauppauge, New York 11788

Library of Congress Catalog Card No. 95-83570

International Standard Book No. 0-8120-9642-8

PRINTED IN HONG KONG
6789 9927 987654321

Read This before You Start

Many people have become interested in astronomy because of the spectacular accomplishments of modern space exploration and because of fascinating celestial events like solar and lunar eclipses. In regions where the air is clear and unpolluted—as in the mountains—and in southern countries, the multitude of stars can often seem so overwhelming that one finds oneself wondering how anyone knows what is what in the night sky.

With this Barron's Mini Fact Finder *Stars:* June 1996–May 1999 Edition you will be able to orient yourself quickly and easily. In it there are 56 maps that show all the stars, constellations, and planets that are visible in different seasons and at different nighttime hours from almost any point on Earth. Wherever you may be, with the help of this pocket-sized guide you will be able to figure out what part of the sky you are seeing at any hour of the night.

The "Introduction to Astronomy" gives you a basic understanding of the amazing interplay between the celestial bodies, even if you have no previous knowledge of astronomy.

This 1996–1999 edition includes the following features:

- Dates of interest from June 1996 through May 1999.
- A table of the lunar phases (page 80) that gives the dates of all the phases: full moon and new moon as well as first quarter and last quarter.
- The spectacular eclipsing of the bright planets by the moon, which occasionally conceals even the distant planets. Each of these rare events, if it is visible in the evening until about two hours after sunset, is mentioned in connection with the relevant star maps.
- A special advantage of this guide is that it fits into any shirt or trouser pocket. This makes it especially suitable for travelers, who will now be able to find the answer to questions concerning the night sky in whatever country they are.

The author and the editors of Barron's Mini Fact Finders wish you much enjoyment and success in exploring the night sky.

The photo on the preceding double page depicts Orion, which is the only constellation that contains not just one but two of the sky's ten brightest stars: Betelgeuse and Rigel. The dark nebula in Orion has been named "Horsehead" because of its shape (on the right side of the picture).

Introduction to Astronomy

Sun, Moon, and Earth

For us, Earth is the most important celestial body. Earth is a spherical object 7,913 miles (12,742 km) in diameter and enveloped by a layer of air (the atmosphere) that, by protecting us from dangerous cosmic radiation, makes life possible for us. Once a day, that is, every 24 hours, Earth rotates around its own axis, which is an imaginary straight line that runs from the north to the south pole. Because of Earth's rotation we see the stars rise in the east and set in the west. In the course of the night the starry sky changes its appearance completely: New stars appear, and others vanish from sight.

The sun is crucial for Earth and its inhabitants. It is a huge, blazing ball of gas, in whose core atomic nuclei are fused in a process that releases energy. Thanks to the incredibly vast amounts of energy thus produced, the sun radiates great quantities of light and heat toward Earth and thus provides the energy that is necessary for life to emerge. The rising and setting of the sun create our days and nights.

When the sun is in the sky during the day, it shines so brightly that all other celestial bodies—which are overhead not just at night but during the day as well—fade from sight. It is only in the evening, when the sun sinks below the horizon and darkness falls, that we can see the other, much less luminous celestial bodies.

The sun's disk frequently displays dark spots. The number of these so-called sunspots fluctuates in an eleven-year cycle. The "solar activity" associated with sunspots was at a low point in 1995. In the years 1996–1999 we will again see more sunspots.

Only one other celestial body is sometimes visible during the day: the moon, which measures 2,159 miles (3,476 km) in diameter and is thus considerably smaller than Earth. The moon revolves around Earth approximately once a month. It is Earth's companion or satellite, a cold celestial body that is inhospitable to life. Humans first set foot on the moon on July 20, 1969. Like Earth, the moon derives its light from the sun, and it reflects this light back to Earth. The moon appears to us in continually changing form as it circles around Earth; and we speak of its "waxing" and "waning" as, in the course of 29 1/2 days, it passes through the different phases of the lunar cycle. The diagram that follows shows how these familiar "lunar phases" come about. Depending on the moon's position in relation to the sun, we see sometimes the entire lit-up side of the moon (full moon); sometimes only half of the lit-up side (half moon); and, when the moon is closest to the sun, we don't see anything at all because the moon turns its unlit side toward us (new moon). A table of the lunar phases is given on page 80.

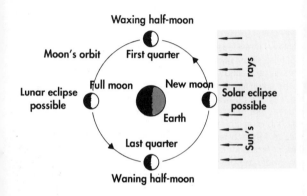

As it revolves around Earth, the moon occasionally produces the most dramatic celestial events we can observe: lunar and solar eclipses. The accompanying diagram shows how eclipses come about. Earth and the moon throw shadows, like any other body that is lit up. When Earth's shadow falls on the moon, we see a lunar eclipse; when the moon's shadow hits Earth, it causes a solar eclipse. Solar eclipses are always visible from only a small part of Earth's surface; lunar eclipses, on the other hand, can be seen on about half of Earth's night

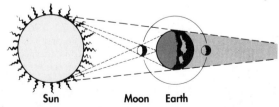

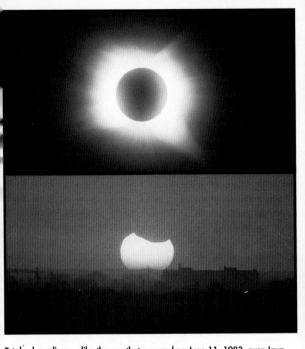

Total solar eclipses—like the one that occurred on June 11, 1983, over Java and depicted in the upper half of the above illustration—leave a deep impression on the observer. In a partial solar eclipse only part of the sun's disk is hidden by the moon while the rest remains visible. The one shown in the lower half of the illustration was photographed in Hamburg, Germany on July 20, 1982.

side. Both lunar and solar eclipses can be total or partial depending on whether the solar or lunar disk is entirely covered up or only partially. In a total solar eclipse we can see the sun's corona for a few minutes. This ring of radiating light consists of highly diffused gases heated to a temperature of several million degrees Celsius, but its luminosity is too small to be seen except during total eclipses.

Solar and lunar eclipses are quite rare, and they are not visible from all parts of Earth. All eclipses between June 1996, and May 1999, both solar and lunar, are briefly described in the text accompanying the star maps.

From Mercury to Pluto

Earth not only rotates around its axis every 24 hours; it also circles around the sun, completing one orbit in exactly one year. But it is not alone on this journey—there are eight other "planets" that also revolve around the central body of what we call our solar system. The planets, listed in order of increasing distance from the sun, are: Mercury, Venus, Earth, Mars, Jupiter, Saturn, Uranus, Neptune, and Pluto. The following mnemonic sentence will help you remember their order: My Very Eager Mother Just Spotted Umpteen New Planets.

The planets differ greatly from each other: Some are considerably larger than Earth, like Jupiter, the biggest of the planets. Some are much hotter, like Mercury, whose proximity to the sun exposes it to the full force of the sun's rays, giving it a surface temperature of 400 degrees Celsius. On some planets it is very cold, as on Pluto, which is 3.6 billion miles (5.9 billion km) away from the sun—that is 40 times the distance between Earth and the sun. On Pluto the temperature reaches a low of minus 230 degrees Celsius. Of the nine planets only five are visible to the unaided eye; to see Uranus, Neptune, and Pluto a telescope is needed. The same is true for the impressive rings of Saturn and for the asteroids or "minor planets," that orbit around the sun by the thousands.

The Jupiter Crash

If the sun were suddenly to disappear, Jupiter, by far the largest of the planets, could force all the other planets to orbit around it. As it is, the planet can exert its gravitational attraction on smaller celestial bodies, such as comets. This is what happened to Shoemaker-Levy 9, a comet that was first discovered in 1992. In July of 1994 fragments of the comet's head (or nucleus) crashed into Jupiter. The first collision occurred on July 16 and the last on July 22. These impacts set off huge explosions in the planet's atmosphere that could be seen clearly from Earth as fireballs around the edges of the planet. Astronomers consider the Jupiter crash a once-in-many-thousand-years event. They compare

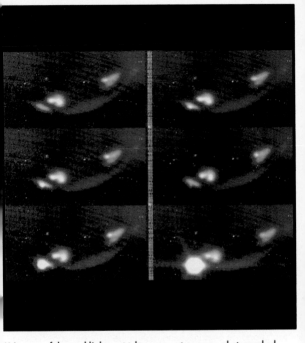

Using one of the world's largest telescopes, astronomers photographed the smashing of a piece of the comet Shoemaker-Levy 9 into Jupiter on July 21, 1994. As recorded on film with infrared exposure, the huge explosion caused Jupiter to flare up suddenly. The impact was so powerful that the comet was completely vaporized in Jupiter's atmosphere and left a hole the size of Earth in the planet's cloudy surface.

it to the crashing into Earth of a meteor or comet some 65 million years ago (which may have caused the extinction of the dinosaurs). The only traces Shoemaker-Levy 9 left behind on Jupiter were some cloud turbulence and holes in the planet's atmosphere, but even these have already disappeared.

Cosmic Bolts of Light

Often during a clear night what we call meteors or shooting stars streak briefly across the sky. These bright and sometimes

9

startling trails of light that spurt across the sky at lightning speed are caused by tiny metallic and rock particles that enter Earth's atmosphere from outer space. The particles become extremely hot, excite the air to incandescence with their great speed, and are incinerated completely in the process. A grain of dust weighing less than one gram can give rise to a meteor that momentarily glows brighter than the brightest stars.

The Fixed Stars

If one looks up at the sky during a clear night and far from the air pollution of cities one has the impression of seeing innumerable stars. In fact, "only" about 2,500 stars are visible to the naked eye. When one looks through binoculars or a telescope, the number of visible stars increases to hundreds of thousands or several million. All the stars rise and set in the sky just like the sun, moon, and planets, because Earth rotates once a day. Apart from this nightly rising and setting, the stars exhibit practically no motion; their position in relation to each other remains essentially constant. Because of this apparent immobility the astronomers of antiquity called them the "fixed stars."

The reason why the stars seem to be glued to their places in the sky is that they are separated from Earth by incredibly vast distances. To illustrate how distance affects our perception of the speed of motion we need only think of a train passing us on the ground and an airplane flying high in the sky overhead. The train seems to move much faster in spite of the fact that the airplane's speed exceeds that of the train by several hundred miles per hour.

The stars are so very far removed from Earth that astronomers had to invent a new unit for measuring distance, the light-year.

One light-year is the distance that light travels (at a speed per second of 186,282 miles or 300,000 km, a distance equal to $7\frac{1}{2}$ times around Earth's equator) in exactly one year. It is equivalent to 5.88 trillion miles (9.46 trillion km). (A trillion is a "1" followed by 12 zeroes.)

How is it possible for us to see stars at all at such incredible, "astronomical" distances? Because they emit huge amounts of heat and light, just like our sun. All fixed stars are suns, some bigger, some smaller than ours.

Fixed stars and planets are therefore two entirely different things. Stars are spheres of incandescent gas that produce their own light; the planets are solid, cold bodies that orbit around the sun and are illuminated by it. The stars are light-years away from us—that is trillions of miles—while the planets move much closer to Earth, being separated from us by "mere" millions or billions of miles. The other big difference between stars and planets is that the latter do not stay in one place in the sky. They revolve around the sun and thus keep changing their positions as seen from Earth, appearing now in one constellation, now in another.

The Constellations

According to Greek mythology, Queen Cassiopeia and her husband Cepheus once ruled over Ethiopia. One day Cassiopeia bragged that their daughter Andromeda was more beautiful than the Nereids, the daughters of the sea god, Nereus. When the Nereids complained to their father about Cassiopeia's arrogance, Nereus sent a sea monster to ravage the shore of Ethiopia. In desperation King Cepheus consulted the oracle of Delphi. There he was told that the only way to save his country was to sacrifice Andromeda to the monster. Andromeda was chained to a rock by the sea. However, salvation came at the last minute in the form of Perseus, who managed to subdue and kill the sea monster in a ferocious battle. As his reward Perseus received Andromeda in marriage and Ethiopia as her dowry. The gods later immortalized all the participants as constellations in the heavens, including the sea monster, which appears there as Cetus, the Whale.

This is just one of many stories told by ancient bards, stories whose protagonists the Greeks thought they recognized in the skies. These ancient people looked for bright stars and combined them in patterns that they then named after legendary figures. In the southern half of the celestial sphere, we find startlingly different names, such as Antlia, the Air Pump. Many of the southern constellations were not named until the eighteenth century, when astronomers no longer had much use for ancient mythology and preferred to elevate the most recent scientific inventions to the heavens—one of which was the air pump.

From a number of different traditions modern astronomers have selected a total of 88 constellations and drawn up internationally recognized boundaries between them. Of these

88 constellations the most obviously visible 57 appear in the star maps of this star guide. Each constellation has its own characteristic shape. Today the constellations no longer have meaning beyond orienting the observer of the starry sky; they constitute a kind of "coordinate grid" of the sky.

The Zodiac

There are twelve constellations that have a special importance: Aries, Taurus, Gemini, Cancer, Leo, Virgo, Libra, Scorpius, Sagittarius, Capricorn, Aquarius, and Pisces—the constellations of the zodiac. Through these constellations runs one of the most important (imaginary) lines used in astronomy as an orientation aid, namely the "ecliptic." The ecliptic is the circle the sun seems to describe around the celestial sphere in the course of a year. In reality it is, of course, Earth that circles around the sun once a year, not the the sun around Earth. But the only way to observe Earth's movement around the sun would be from a point outside the solar system. When we look at the sun from where we are, it seems as though the sun travels along the celestial sphere. This apparent journey takes the sun through the constellations of the zodiac, precisely along the line of the ecliptic. It is because of the sun's apparent movement that some constellations are visible only during the summer and others only during winter. Thus, when the sun is in front of Leo's stars, this constellation rises in the morning along with the sun. All the stars in and around Leo travel across the sky along with the sun during the day. We cannot see them because the sun's brilliant light obliterates the more modest gleam of the stars. In the evening Leo's stars drop below the western horizon along with the sun and are thus not visible during the night either. Not until six months later, when the sun has moved away from Leo and is on the opposite side of the sky in the constellation Capricorn, do Leo and its neighbors rise in the east as the sun sets in the west, and now we can watch them in the night sky. Because the sun repeats its apparent journey annually with great precision, we always see the same stars and constellations every year at any given month or day.

The moon and all the planets also move along the ecliptic. The ecliptic is therefore also important in watching these celestial bodies. They appear to us always only along this

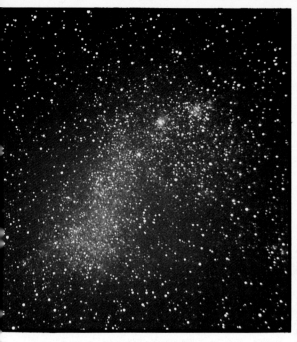

The Large Magellanic Cloud (LMC) and the Small Magellanic Cloud (SMC), are among the galaxies that are closest to Earth.

imaginary line, that is, in front of the zodiacal constellations. The phrase "in front of" literally refers to a spacial relationship, for the planets, as we have already seen, are only millions or at most a few billion miles away from us, whereas the fixed stars are many trillions of miles distant.)

The Galaxies

One of the most imposing celestial sights is the Milky Way, a band of light produced by billions of stars. The single stars, if they each stood isolated in the sky, would be too faint to be seen, but all of them together combine into a band of shimmering light. Interspersed among these billions of stars are

13

clouds of dark dust that in places block the light from reaching Earth and give the Milky Way an uneven, ragged look. The universe includes more than the Milky Way; there are innumerable other, similar formations in space that are made up of stars and dust and gasses; each formation is a "galaxy" like our Milky Way. ("Galaxy" and "Milky Way" have the same meaning since gala is Greek for "milk.") One of these galaxies is the Large Magellanic Cloud in the southern sky, visible to the naked eye even at full moon as a large, misty area. When viewed through a telescope it turns out to be a huge aggregation of stars. The Magellanic Clouds (there is a small as well as a large one) are named after the navigator Magellan. The Large Magellanic Cloud is the galaxy closest to us at a distance of about 150,000 light-years. Astronomers estimate that it contains approximately 15 to 30 billion stars. It also includes many nebulae, star clusters, and other objects that show up in varied colors in photographs of the clouds (see photo, page 13).

In 1987 a supernova (technical name: 1987A) was discovered in the Large Magellanic Cloud, the latest one to be visible to the unaided eye. This supernova aroused particular interest because it was the first to be observed with the most modern and sophisticated instruments. Thanks to this up-to-date equipment, astronomers succeeded in detecting an unusual signal emitted during this celestial explosion: the arrival of neutrons traveling at the speed of light.

All the galaxies together—many of them millions or billions of light-years away—make up the universe, which today's astronomers can explore with a vast array of instruments: radio telescopes like the 300-foot (100 m) antenna in Effelsberg/Eifel; sophisticated mirror telescopes like the one at the European Observatory in Chile that can cancel out air disturbances automatically; Voyager 2, the most successful space probe launched thus far; and the Hubble space telescope, which is able to photograph distant celestial bodies with previously unattainable accuracy.

Table of Planets and Stars

The Planets

Name	Distance from sun in mill. miles/(km)	Diameter miles/(km)	Mass*	Number of satellites
Mercury	36 (57.9)	3,006 (4,840)	.05	—
Venus	67.2 (108.2)	7,517 (12,104)	.81	—
Earth	92.9 (149.6)	7,913 (12,742)	1	1
Mars	141.5 (227.9)	4,219 (6,794)	.11	2
Jupiter	483 (778)	88,672 (142,790)	318	16
Saturn	886 (1,427)	74,520 (120,000)	95	17
Uranus	1,782 (2,870)	31,547 (50,800)	14	15
Neptune	2,792 (4,496)	30,180 (48,600)	17	8
Pluto	3,666 (5,900)	1,400 (2,250)	.002	1

*In multiples of Earth's mass: 1 = 5,976 quadrillion tons

The Ten Brightest Stars

Name	Constellation	Distance from Earth (in light years)	Mass*	Diameter (Multiple of sun's diam.)
(Sun)	—	(92.9 mill. miles/ 149.6 mill. km)	1	(.87 mill. m. / 1.4 mill. km)
Sirius	Canis Major (see p. 55)	8.9	3	1.7
Canopus	Carina (see p. 77)	370	12	60
Toliman Alpha Centauri)	Centaurus (see p. 76)	4.2	1	1
Arcturus	Boötes (see p.35)	36	4	26
Vega	Lyra (see p. 59)	26	4	3
Capella	Auriga (see p. 38)	46	3	16
Rigel	Orion (see p. 58)	1,300	30	19
Procyon	Canis Minor (see p. 58)	11	2	2
Achernar	Eridanus (see p. 74)	78	6	9
Altair	Aquila (see p. 54)	16	2	1.6

*Multiples of the sun's mass: 1 = 2,000 septillion tons

Using the Star Maps

Astronomers have divided the celestial sphere that seems to surround us into two halves that are analogous to Earth's northern and southern hemispheres. There is also a celestial north and a celestial south pole—they lie on the extended axis that runs through Earth's north and south poles—and a celestial equator. Thus, just as we have northern and southern countries on Earth, there are northern and southern constellations in the sky. Only one half of the celestial sphere is visible from any one point on Earth; the other half lies below the circle of the horizon. Each star map shows the half of the celestial sphere that is visible at the latitude and in the month indicated.

What the Maps Show

All the maps show only "fixed" stars. These stars are classified into three groups according to their brightness: The faintest are represented by the smallest dots, the brightest, by the biggest. In the hazy skies lit up by city lights the brightest are practically the only stars one can detect, and they are also the ones that show up first as dusk falls. The names that appear in the round star maps are those of constellations, and the main stars making up a constellation are connected by lines so that the characteristic shapes of the constellations can be quickly identified (see inside front cover). Once you have gained an overview of the stars in the sky with the help of the round maps, you may want to find out a little more about some individual stars and constellations. That is why at the end of each map series the most important constellations are briefly presented. Here you will find the names of especially bright stars. To facilitate finding the constellations in the sky, the diagrams include directional arrows pointing to the celestial north pole (NP) or the celestial south pole (SP): The same letters also appear on the round maps so that you can look for the constellations in their proper positions. The ecliptic that appears in the round maps is, of course, an imaginary line, but the maps show it as a line passing near certain bright stars to help you picture it in the sky. The Milky Way is represented by a whitish area, and its dark parts are also indicated.

How to Use the Maps

If you face north (N), east (E) lies on your right and west (W) on your left. On the maps, east and west appear reversed. The reason for this is as follows: Each map shows the celestial hemisphere above you, and, in order to compare it to the stars overhead, you would have to hold it above your head. Try doing this once, making sure the N on the map points north. You will see that E and W point in the correct directions.

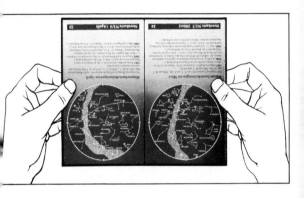

But in actual practice, reading star maps this way is very awkward, and the usual way is to hold the map vertically in front of you with the direction of the sky you want to observe pointing downward. Thus, if you want to watch the eastern sky, hold the map so that E is at the bottom, or, if you face north, N is at the bottom. You may be holding the book sideways or upside down (picture above), but what you see overhead exactly matches the part of the map above the letter indicating direction (as shown on the inside front cover)—and that is what counts!

Determining the points of the compass is quite easy. In the northern hemisphere the Big Dipper and Polaris—the latter always shines in the north—help you get oriented (see page 37). How to find the south celestial pole in the southern

17

hemisphere, where there is no polar star, is explained in connection with the map S/February (see page 70).

Where the Maps Apply

What stars are visible depends (apart from the time of day and year) on the geographic latitude of the location from which you are observing the sky. In this star guide the views of the sky are grouped in three categories—one for 50 degrees north latitude (N I), one for 30 degrees north latitude (N II), and one for 20 degrees south latitude (S). Your point of observation may deviate from these meridians by as much as 10 degrees in either direction without the view of the sky changing significantly. This star guide thus can be used in almost all parts of the world. Just look in the geographical maps (page 21, 41, or 61) for the place where you are located.

When the Maps Are Valid

Each of the round star maps depicts the sky for the month given in big print at the bottom of the page. The sky is shown as it appears at 9:30 P.M. at the beginning of the month, at 8:30 P.M. in the middle of the month, and at 7:30 P.M. at the end of the month. You don't have to pay too close attention to the exact times; if you want to watch the stars anytime between 8 and 10 P.M., just find the correct month given at the bottom of each map page.

In states and countries that observe daylight saving time, the clocks are set ahead an hour for the period from April to October. For stargazing, the practical consequence of daylight saving time is that for the maps of series N I and N II the times of validity are shifted during the summer to 10:30 P.M. for the beginning, 9:30 P.M. for the middle, and 8:30 P.M. for the end of the month, that is, to between approximately 9 and 11 P.M. In the southern hemisphere the seasons come at different times of the calendar year. When we have summer, it is winter there. If you plan to use the star maps of series S you should inquire whether summer or winter time is in effect in the place where you wish to stargaze.

Keep in mind that the transitions from one month to the next are gradual. This is important especially for the last and very first days of the month. If, for instance, you want to identify stars at 11 P.M. on July 30, you should consult the map for August because it applies for the beginning of August at 10:30 P.M. Conversely, for watching the stars around 8:45 P.M. on May 3, the map for April is recommended because it shows what the sky looks like at the end of April around 8:30 P.M.

If you want to stargaze at a time of night other than between 8 and 10 P.M. (9 and 11 P.M. during daylight saving time), turn to the table on the inside back cover. Find the month you are interested in at the top and the hour of night in the left-hand column: Where the vertical and the horizontal lines intersect, you will be directed to the correct map to use.

Let us look at an example: You would like to identify the stars in Texas (the geographical map on page 41 shows that map series N II applies here) on July 10 at 1 A.M. In July, daylight saving time is in effect. This means you have to subtract an hour from what your watch says and look under 12:00 P.M. Where the column "Beginning of July" and the horizontal line "11 and 12 P.M." intersect, you find the number 3; therefore map N II/August on page 44 applies.

Another example: You are in North Dakota and want to find out where Orion can be found on December 28 at 4:30 A.M. December 28 can be considered the beginning of January, and at the intersection of the appropriate row and column you find—nothing. The missing section of the sky lies between the maps for May and April, and we therefore turn to map N /May on page 33, and, if we are interested in a star close to the horizon, we may also want to look at map N I/April. Don't worry about the fact that the maps you are using are labeled August (in the first example) and May (in the second) even though you are watching the sky in July and in December. The indicated months apply only for the usual stargazing time of 8 to 10 P.M. (or, during daylight saving time, 9 to 11 P.M.).

The Planets

The planets and the moon do not appear in the star maps because they move across the sky so quickly that their course would have to be entered anew every year. When looking for planets, what we have to go on is that they (and the moon) always are to be found near the ecliptic, which is marked on every map. And since only the zodiacal constellations are located on the ecliptic (see page 11), those are the only

19

constellation names you will find in notes referring to the planets. These notes mention what planets can be seen where in the evening (until about midnight) and, in parentheses, in the morning (after midnight). In the maps of series N I and N II all the indicated times from April through September have already been translated into daylight saving time.

Let us look at an example: In 1997 the planet Saturn becomes visible in June between the parallels of 40 and 60 degrees north latitude (map series N II) in the constellation Pisces at 4 A.M. (see page 42). In June, daylight saving time is in effect. We therefore have to subtract an hour before consulting the table on the inside back cover. Now, if we read across from "3 to 4 A.M." to the column for June, we find that map N II/9 (page 45) applies. On this map the ecliptic runs through the constellations Sagittarius, Capricornus, Aquarius, and Pisces toward the northern horizon. Saturn consequently must appear there, on the ecliptic, in the constellation Pisces, at 4 A.M. daylight saving time.

And, finally, a few pointers to help you tell which shining points in the sky are which planets:

● Generally, all planets appear very bright and can be mistaken only for the very brightest stars. The light of planets does not flicker but appears clear and steady.

● Mercury is the most difficult planet to observe. It shows up for a maximum of only one hour—low in the western sky right after sunset or in the east before sunrise.

● Venus, too, can be seen only after sunset in the west, when it appears as the "evening star," or else before sunrise in the east as the "morning star." It is the most luminous of all the celestial bodies (except for the moon and the sun).

● Mars is easy to recognize by its red color (more a reddish tint than a true red). Because of its color it is often referred to as the "red planet."

● Jupiter always appears very bright (brighter than Mars and Saturn but fainter than Venus) and shines with an unmistakable yellowish light.

● Saturn's light, finally, is a neutral white. From 1996 through 1999 this planet will constantly remain near the stars of the constellations Pisces and Aries.

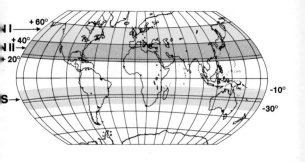

Star Maps and Constellations

The maps in Series N I are for the latitudes between 40 and 60
degrees north. They are applicable for the northern United
States, Canada, and the countries of northern, central, and
eastern Europe—that is, the Benelux countries, Scandinavia,
Germany, Austria, Switzerland, northern Italy, France, Great
Britain, Poland, Czechoslovakia, Hungary, Romania, the former
Yugoslavia, Bulgaria, and for the countries of the former USSR.

Reminders

If you travel to areas farther south, turn to the map series N II
(see page 41). Should you want to identify stars north of 60
degrees north latitude, you will notice that the stars in the south
are lower and those in the north higher in the sky. The
positions of the stars and constellations in relation to each
other remain unchanged.

From April through October, daylight saving time is in effect
in many countries. The positions of the planets are therefore
given in terms of daylight saving time for these months.

In regions north of 55 degrees north latitude, the nights are
not dark enough during the summer for observing stars. This is
the period of twilight nights and, north of the Arctic Circle, of
the midnight sun. There, the sun stays in the sky 24 hours a
day at this time of year.

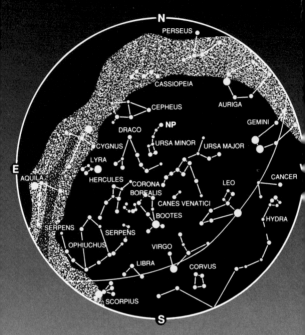

Celestial Events during June

Summer officially begins on June 20 at 9 P.M. in 1996, on June 21 at 3 A.M. in 1997, and on the same date in 1998, this time at 9 A.M.

1996: Jupiter appears around midnight in Sagittarius. (Mercury, Mars, and Venus show up very close together low on the northeastern horizon shortly before sunrise.)

1997: Mars is in Leo and in Virgo. (Jupiter appears about 1 A.M. in Capricorn; Saturn, about 4 A.M. in Pisces in the east.)

1998: There are no planets in the evening sky. (Jupiter can be seen from midnight on and Saturn from 2 A.M. on in the eastern sky. Jupiter is in Aquarius; Saturn, in Aries. Venus appears in the eastern sky, in Taurus, about four hours before sunrise.)

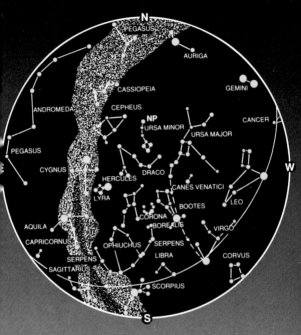

Celestial Events during July

During this month the distance between Earth and the sun grows to its annual maximum. The maximum distance is reached on the 5th in 1996, on the 4th in 1997, and on the 4th in 1998.

1996: On the 4th, Jupiter is in its best annual viewing position, in Sagittarius. (Saturn can be seen in Pisces from 1 A.M. on in the eastern sky; and Venus, in close proximity to Mars, appears around 3 A.M. in Taurus in the eastern sky.)

1997: Venus appears as the "evening star" in the western sky. Mars is in Virgo; Jupiter, in Capricorn. (From about 1 A.M. on Saturn is in Pisces in the eastern sky.)

1998: Jupiter is visible from midnight on in the east, in the constellations Aquarius and Pisces. (Saturn appears around 1 A.M. in Aries in the eastern sky. Venus can be seen briefly in Taurus shortly before sunrise.)

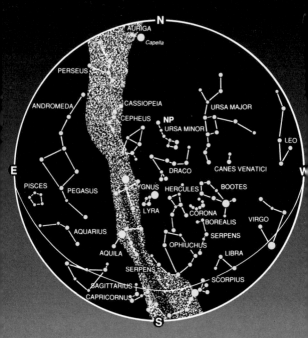

Celestial Events during August

From the 8th through the 13th large numbers of shooting stars, or meteors, emanate from Perseus; this meteor shower is known as the Perseids or the "Tears of Lawrence."

1996: Jupiter is in Sagittarius; Saturn, in Pisces. (Before sunrise Venus shines very brightly in the east, in the constellation Gemini; on the 20th, it is in its best position in relation to the sun; Mars, much dimmer, may also be seen just before sunrise.)

1997: Jupiter is in Capricorn, where it attains its best annual position in relation to the sun on the 9th. Mars is in Virgo; Saturn, in Pisces; and Venus, in the constellations Leo and Virgo.

1998: Jupiter is in Pisces; Saturn, in Aries in the eastern sky from 11 P.M. on.

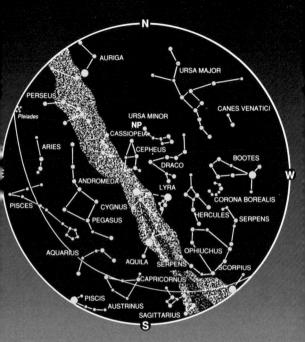

Celestial Events during September

Fall begins at 1 P.M. on September 22 in 1996, 7 p.m. on September 22 in 1997, and 2 A.M. on September 23 in 1998.

1996: September 14 marks the beginning of the year 5757 in the Jewish calendar. On the 26th there is a total lunar eclipse (8:15 P.M. to 11:37 P.M.) over North and South America and over western and eastern Europe. On the 26th, Saturn is in its best annual viewing position, in Pisces; Jupiter is in Sagittarius. (On the 4th, Venus and Mars appear very close together in the morning in the eastern sky, in Cancer.)

1997: On the 16th a total lunar eclipse (12:10 P.M. to 3:25 P.M.) is visible from Russia and Europe. Venus and Mars are in Libra; Jupiter is in Capricorn; and Saturn, in Pisces.

1998: The new Jewish year starts on September 21. On the 16th, Jupiter is in its best annual viewing position, in Aquarius and Pisces. Saturn is in Aries.

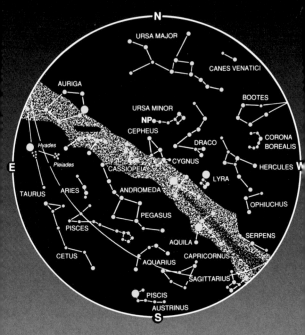

Celestial Events during October

In most countries daylight saving time ends in this month. The clocks are set back one hour.

1996: On the 12th a partial solar eclipse occurs over Europe and northern Africa. It is visible in Germany, Austria, and Switzerland. Saturn is in Pisces; Jupiter, in Sagittarius. (Mars is in Leo from 3 A.M. on, and Venus appears about 4 A.M.)

1997: October 2 marks the beginning of the year 5758 according to the Jewish calendar. On the 9th, Saturn is in its best viewing position of the year, in Pisces. Jupiter is in Capricorn. On the 26th, Mars and Venus can be seen close together low in the western sky.)

1998: On the 23rd, Saturn is in its best viewing position of the year in Aries. Jupiter is in Aquarius. (Mars can be seen from 3 A.M. on in Leo in the eastern sky.)

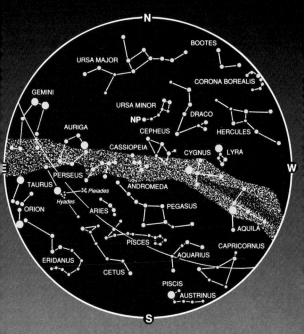

Celestial Events during November

1996: Jupiter can be seen at dusk in the southwest; Saturn is in Pisces. (From 1 A.M. on Mars is in Leo in the northeastern sky; Venus shines in the southeastern sky from 4 A.M. on in the constellation Virgo.)

1997: On the 6th, Venus is in its best annual position in relation to the sun; it appears in the evening together with Mars in the constellation Sagittarius. Jupiter is in Capricorn; Saturn, in Pisces.

1998: Jupiter is in Pisces; Saturn, in Aries. (From 2 A.M. on Mars is in the eastern sky in the constellation Leo.) On the 17th an exceptionally large number of meteors may be seen in the constellation Leo, the so-called Leonids. This meteor shower is caused by the encounter of an unusually dense dust cloud with Earth's atmosphere.

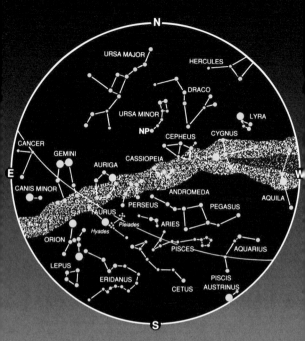

Celestial Events during December

Winter officially begins at 9 A.M. on the 21st in 1996, at 3 P.M. on the 21st in 1997, and at 9 P.M. on the 21st in 1998. At these times the sun passes through its southernmost point on the ecliptic.

1996: Saturn is in Pisces. (Mars can be seen in the east in Leo from 1 A.M. on, and Venus appears shortly before sunrise.)

1997: On the 22nd, Mars and Venus draw close together low in the western sky. Jupiter can be seen in the west in Capricorn until about 8 P.M. Saturn is in Pisces.

1998: Jupiter is in Pisces; Saturn, in Aries. (From 1 A.M. on, Mars is visible in Virgo in the eastern sky.)

Star Map N 1/December — 28

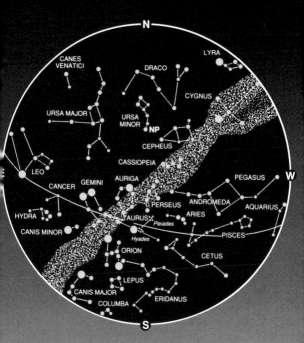

Celestial Events during January

The distance between Earth and the sun reaches its annual minimum: "only" 91.3 million miles (147.1 million km). This occurs on January 1 in 1997, on January 4 in 1998, and on January 3 in 1999.

1997: Saturn is in Pisces. (Mars can be seen in the east, in Virgo, after midnight.)

1998: According to the Chinese and Japanese calendar, the Year of the Tiger starts on January 28. Saturn is in Pisces. Mars and Jupiter can be seen close together low in the western sky after sunset.

1999: Venus can be seen shining brightly in the west during the early evening twilight. Early in the month, Jupiter moves from Aquarius to join Saturn in Pisces. (Mars rises after midnight in the east where it can be seen for the rest of the night in Virgo.)

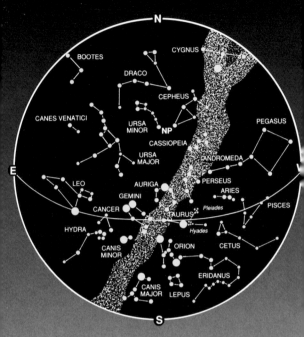

Celestial Events during February

1997: According to the Chinese and Japanese calendar, the Year of the Ox starts on February 7. Saturn is in Pisces; Mars, in Virgo in the eastern sky after 11 P.M.

1998: Mars and Jupiter are very low in the western sky at dusk. (Starting at the end of February, Venus shines in the east, in the constellation Sagittarius, as the "morning star.")

1999: Jupiter and Venus can be found low in the west after sunset. Saturn is in Pisces. (Mars, visible after midnight, moves from Virgo into Libra late in the month.)

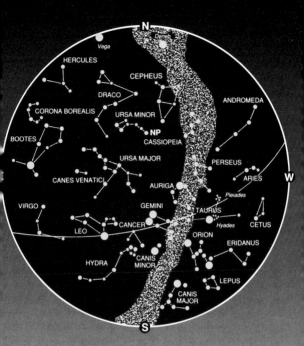

Celestial Events during March

Spring officially begins on March 20th at 9 A.M. in 1997, on the 20th at 3 P.M. in 1998, and on the 20th at 9 P.M. in 1999.

1997: On the 8th there is a total solar eclipse over eastern Russia and over China. On the 23rd a partial lunar eclipse (from 10:00 P.M. to 1:21 A.M.) is visible from Canada, the United States, and Europe. On the 17th, Mars is in Leo, in its best viewing position of the year.

1998: There are no planets visible in the evening sky. (Venus appears in the morning; on the 27th it is in its best position in relation to the sun, in the constellation Capricorn.)

1999: Venus shines as the bright "evening star" in the west at sunset. Saturn is above it, much fainter and a bit to the south. Both planets start the month in the constellation Pisces and move into Aries during March. Mars, in Libra rises around 10:30 P.M.

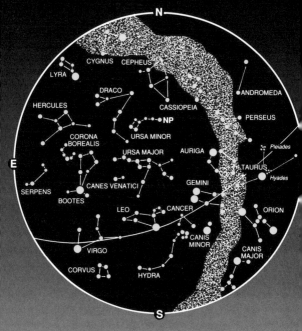

Celestial Events during April

During April daylight saving time goes into effect in many countries. The clocks are set ahead one hour.

1997: Mars is in Leo. (Jupiter appears at 5 A.M. in Capricorn in the east.)

1998: There are no planets in the evening sky. (At dawn, Venus and Jupiter are very close together in the eastern sky.)

1999: Venus is the bright "evening star" high in the west at sunset. Mars has made a loop back into Virgo and rises about 8:30 P.M. On the 24th, it will be in its best viewing position of the year. No other planets are visible until the end of the month when Jupiter begins to appear low in the morning twilight.

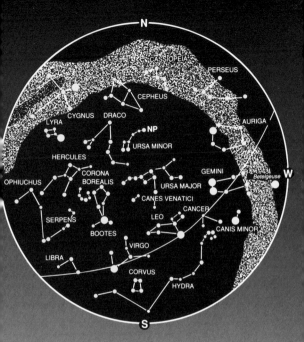

Celestial Events during May

1997: Mars is in Leo. (From 3 A.M. on, Jupiter can be seen in Capricorn in the eastern sky.)

1998: There are no planets visible in the evening sky. (At dawn Venus and Jupiter appear close together in the eastern sky; at the end of the month, Saturn joins them to form an unusual trinity of planets in the constellation Pisces.)

1999: Venus and Mars are both well placed for observing this month. Venus can be found high in the west shining brilliantly with an unmistakable white light. Mars in Virgo is almost equally high in the southeast and glows a bright orange color. (Shortly before sunrise Jupiter appears low in the eastern sky.)

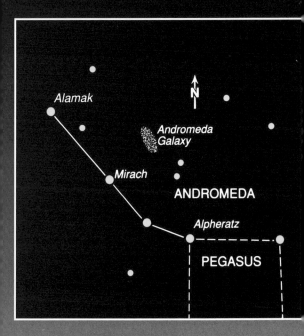

Andromeda

In any discussion of Andromeda, the most famous object in the constellation is bound to be mentioned, namely, the Andromeda Galaxy. Its technical name is M 31. (M stands for Charles Messier, an eighteenth century French astronomer who compiled a consecutively numbered catalog of celestial objects that appeared nebulous—hence M 31.) The Andromeda Galaxy is the third closest major galaxy after the two Magellanic Clouds (see color photo on page 13). It is composed of over 400 billion stars that are arranged in a huge spiral. The Andromeda Galaxy is 2.7 million light-years away from Earth. We highly recommend that you observe it through binoculars on some clear night.

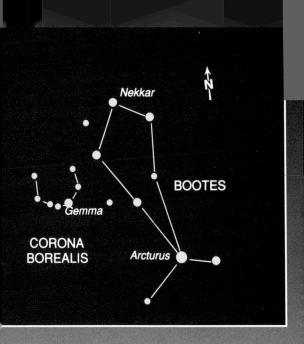

oötes (the Herdsman) and Corona Borealis the Northern Crown)

he constellation Boötes contains the brightest star of the northern celestial emisphere, namely, Arcturus, which stands out because of its reddish color. A tip on how to find Arcturus easily is given in connection with the star map N 1/July (see page 23). Every light ray from Arcturus that reaches us here on Earth has traveled through space for 36 years. Astronomers express this by saying the star is 36 light-years away; this is equivalent to 211 trillion miles (340 trillion km)!

The Northern Crown has a counterpart in the southern celestial hemisphere (see page 79). But the Northern Crown includes an exceptionally brilliant jewel, the star Gemma (Latin for "jewel"). The Southern Crown has nothing comparable to offer. Gemma is 71 light-years away from Earth.

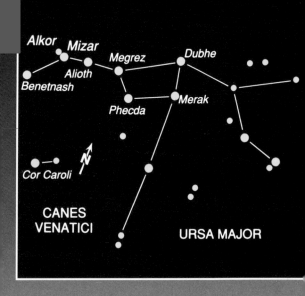

Ursa Major (the Great Bear) and Canes Venatici (the Hunting Dogs)

Ursa Major is among the best known constellations of the northern sky. Its seven brightest stars—all with sonorous names—make up the Big Dipper, which is not, however, an officially recognized constellation by itself. Make sure to have a good look at the star Mizar; it is often said to be a good test of one's eyesight. Right next to Mizar you may be able, if your eyes are good, to spot Alcor, which means "little charioteer." In Europe the Big Dipper is often referred to as the "Big Wagon," and Alcor, the "little charioteer" is said to ride on the horses that are harnessed to the wagon shaft (the handle of the Big Dipper).

For all practical purposes Canes Venatici has only one bright star, Cor Caroli, which means "heart of Charles." Edmond Halley, the astronomer, named this star in 1725 in honor of King Charles II of England.

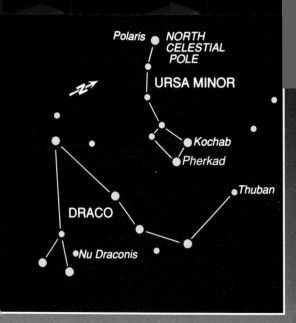

Ursa Minor (the Little Bear) and Draco (the Dragon)

The most famous star in Ursa Minor is Polaris, the north star. It marks the north celestial pole like a beacon, though, as the map shows, it is not positioned exactly on the pole. But its being off the mark by one degree is of no great consequence to the stargazer. Once you spot Polaris in the sky you know where north is. The constellation Draco is not nearly as prominent. But if you have a pair of binoculars you will be able to tell quite clearly that the star Nu Draconis is a double star, or binary. Nu Draconis consists of two stars that lie close to each other, evolve around each other, and look to the naked eye like a single star.

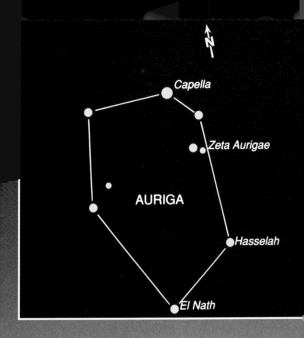

Auriga (the Charioteer)

The most interesting star in Auriga is not the one that shines most brightly, Capella, but Zeta Aurigae. It may sound incredible, but Zeta Aurigae can be "X rayed," and this is how we know that it consists of two separate stars. One of them is 293 times larger than the sun; the other is only five times the sun's size. The two stars revolve around each other, and because the smaller is so tiny in comparison to its larger brother it acts like an X-ray lamp when it disappears behind the bigger star every $2^1/_2$ years. An examination of the light rays has given us some highly interesting information on the structure of the giant star. The star El Nath, though included in the figure of Auriga, is actually part of the constellation Taurus.

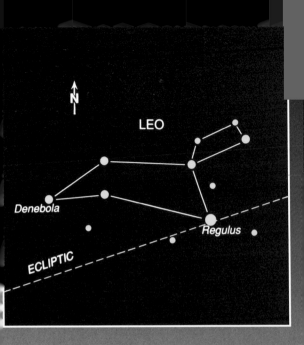

Leo (the Lion)

The constellation Leo is particularly easy to locate in the sky. Its stars form two trapezoids that can readily be imagined to represent a lion. According to Greek myth this lion was of monstrous strength and could be slain only by Hercules. The star Regulus ("little king") counts among the twenty brightest stars of the sky and is four times bigger than the sun. It is 68 light-years away from Earth. Together with Spica (see page 56) and Antares (see page 79) it is among the brightest stars that lie exactly on the ecliptic. That is why planets are often seen near these stars (see page 19).

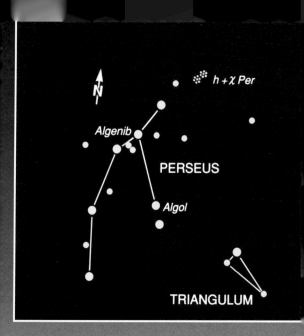

Perseus

Algol, the "demon star," is one of the most interesting stars in the sky. Although it looks like a single star not only to the naked eye but also through a telescope, it in fact consists of two stars that revolve around each other, mutually eclipsing each other every $2^{1}/_{2}$ days. When one star is in front of the other their combined brightness decreases, of course, and Algol is therefore called an "eclipsing variable." The fluctuations in brightness can be noticed even by the unaided eye.

The double star cluster h and chi Persei should really be observed through binoculars. Both clusters, which are 8,000 light-years away from us, are quite spectacular. (Star clusters are aggregations of a few hundred to several thousand stars.)

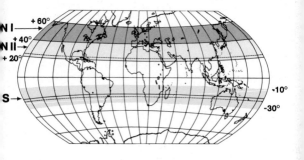

Star Maps and Constellations

The maps in Series N II are for the latitudes between 20 and 40 degrees north. Applicable in the United States, Mexico, the Caribbean, southern Europe, including Spain, Portugal, southern Italy, and Greece; also for Turkey, Lebanon, Israel, Egypt, Tunisia, Algeria, Morocco, Persia, Pakistan, Afghanistan, India, Thailand, Myanmar, China, Korea, Japan, and Taiwan.

Reminders

In these countries the constellations of the southern celestial hemisphere become visible, such as the Southern Cross (see N I/May, page 53). The closer you are to the equator, the more clearly you will be able to see these constellations in the southern sky. From April through October, daylight saving time (DST) is in effect in many countries. Therefore the positions of the planets are given in daylight saving time for this period. The closer you are to the equator, the faster darkness will fall in the evening and the earlier you will be able to see the stars and the planets. Dusk is much briefer in the tropics than in regions farther north or south of the equator. The sun as well as all the other heavenly bodies rise and set more vertically and therefore rise and set more quickly.

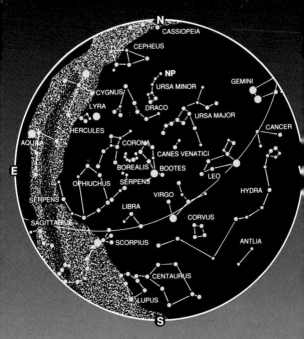

Celestial Events during June

Summer officially begins on June 20 in 1996 and on June 21 in 1997 and 1998.

1996: Jupiter is in Sagittarius. (Mercury, Mars, and Venus can be seen very close together above the northeastern horizon from 5 A.M. on.)

1997: Mars is in Leo and Virgo. (Jupiter is in Capricorn from 1 A.M. on; Saturn, in Pisces in the east from 4 A.M. on.)

1998: There are no planets in the evening sky. (Jupiter can be seen from 2 A.M. on and Saturn from 3 A.M. on in the east; Jupiter, in Aquarius and Saturn in Aries. Venus is visible for about two hours before sunrise.)

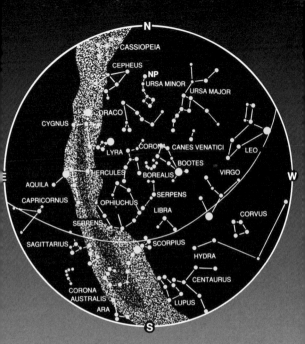

Celestial Events during July

The distance between Earth and the sun is at its maximum during this month: 94.4 million miles (152.1 million km).

1996: On the 4th, Jupiter is in its best viewing position of the year in Sagittarius. (Saturn can be seen from 2 A.M. on in Pisces in the eastern sky. At 4 A.M. Venus also appears in the east, close together with Mars, in the constellation Taurus.)

1997: Venus is in the west in the evening; Mars, in Virgo; and Jupiter, in Capricorn. (Saturn can be seen from 1 A.M. on in Pisces in the eastern sky.)

1998: Jupiter is visible from 11 P.M. on in the east in the constellations Aquarius and Pisces. (Saturn is in Aries in the eastern sky from 2 A.M. on, and Venus shines in the east, in the constellation Taurus, from 4 A.M. on.)

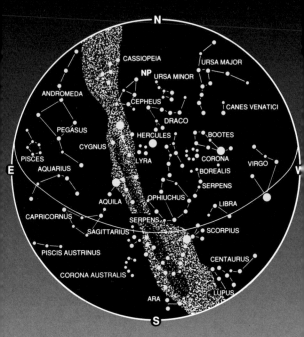

Celestial Events during August

1996: Jupiter is in Sagittarius; Saturn, in Pisces. (Venus shines very brightly in the east in the constellation Gemini before sunrise; on the 20th it is in its best position in relation to the sun.)

1997: On the 9th, Jupiter is in its best viewing position of the year in Capricorn. Mars is in Virgo; Saturn, in Pisces; and Venus, in Leo and Virgo.

1998: On the 21st there is an annular solar eclipse over Indonesia that is visible as a partial eclipse from the southeastern Pacific and the Philippines. Jupiter is in Pisces; Saturn, from 11 P.M. on, in Aries in the eastern sky. (In late August and early September Mercury is visible in the eastern sky before sunrise.)

Celestial Events during September

1996: September 14 marks the beginning of the year 5757 according to the Jewish calendar. On the 26th there is a total lunar eclipse that is visible from Central and North America. Saturn is in its best viewing position of the year on the 26th, in Pisces. Jupiter is in Sagittarius. (Venus and Mars can be seen very close together on the 4th from 4 A.M. on in Cancer in the eastern sky.)

1997: On the 16th there is a total lunar eclipse over Asia, Africa, and Arabia. Venus and Mars are in Libra; Jupiter is in Capricorn; and Saturn, in Pisces. (Mercury can be seen in the eastern sky before sunrise from the 5th to the 25th of the month.)

1998: September 21 marks the beginning of the year 5759 according to the Jewish calendar. On the 16th, Jupiter appears in its best viewing position of the year in the constellations Aquarius and Pisces. Saturn is in Aries.

Celestial Events during October

Starting this month, daylight saving time is no longer in effect in most countries. The clocks are set back one hour.

1996: Saturn is in Pisces; Jupiter, in Sagittarius. (Mars and Venus can both be seen in Leo in the eastern sky, Mars from 4 A.M. and Venus from 5 A.M. on. From October 1 to 15, Mercury appears low in the eastern sky for one hour before the sun rises.)

1997: October 2 marks the beginning of the year 5758 according to the Jewish calendar. On the 9th, Saturn is in its best viewing position of the year in the constellation Pisces. Jupiter is in Capricorn, and on the 26th Mars and Venus can be seen close together low in the western sky.

1998: On the 23rd, Saturn is in its best viewing position of the year in the constellation Aries. Jupiter is in Aquarius. (Mars is in Leo in the eastern sky from 4 A.M. on.)

Celestial Events during November

1996: Jupiter can be seen at dusk in the southwest. Saturn is in Pisces. Mars is in the northeast, in the constellation Leo, from 3 A.M. on, and Venus appears one hour later in the southeast, in Virgo.)

1997: On the 6th, Venus is in its best position in relation to the sun, shining brightly in the western sky together with Mars in the constellation Sagittarius. Jupiter is in Capricorn; Saturn, in Pisces.

1998: Jupiter is in Pisces; Saturn, in Aries. (Mars appears at 3 A.M. in the east in the constellation Leo.) On the 17th there may be an unusually plentiful meteor shower in Leo (the Leonids) caused by Earth's encounter with an especially dense dust cloud.

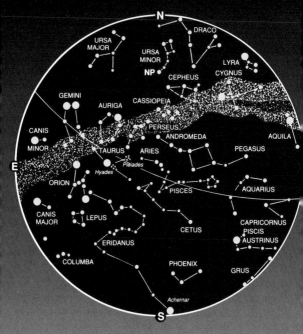

Celestial Events during December

Winter officially starts on the 21st in 1996, 1997, and 1998. The sun at this time reaches the southernmost point on the ecliptic.

1996: Saturn is in Pisces. (Mars is in the eastern sky, in the constellation Leo, from 2 A.M. on. Venus makes its appearance shortly before sunrise.)

1997: On the 22nd there is a close encounter between Mars and Venus low in the western sky. Jupiter is in Capricorn; Saturn, in Pisces.

1998: Jupiter is in Pisces; Saturn, in Aries. (Mars is in the eastern sky from 1 A.M. on, in the constellation Virgo.)

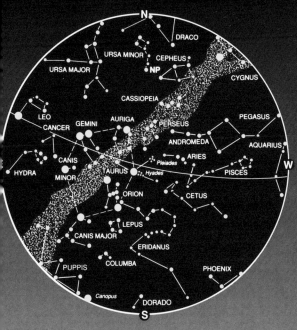

Celestial Events during January

Look for the winter hexagon (indicated by a broken line), which is made up of the brightest stars belonging to Orion, Taurus, Auriga, Gemini, Canis Minor, and Canis Major. The distance between Earth and the sun is at its annual minimum: 91.3 million miles (147.1 million km).

1997: Saturn is in Pisces. (After midnight Mars is in Virgo.)

1998: According to the Chinese and Japanese calendar, the Year of the Tiger begins on January 28. Saturn is in Pisces. After sunset, Mars and Jupiter can be seen very close together low in the western sky. (At the beginning of the month, Mercury makes a brief appearance in the east shortly before sunrise.)

1999: Venus can be seen shining brightly in the early evening twilight in the west. Early in the month, Jupiter moves from Aquarius to join Saturn in Pisces. (Mars rises after midnight in the east where it can be seen for the rest of the night in Virgo.)

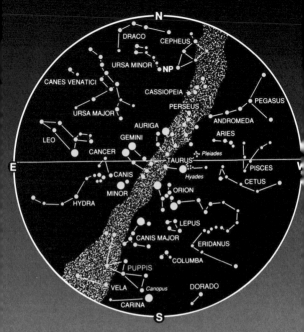

Celestial Events during February

1997: February 7 marks the beginning of the Year of the Ox according to the Chinese and Japanese calendar. Saturn is in Pisces, and Mars appears in the eastern sky, at 11 P.M., in the constellation Virgo.

1998: On the 26th there is a total solar eclipse over Venezuela; it appears as a partial eclipse over Central America and the southern United States. At dusk Mars and Jupiter are low in the western sky, very close together. (From the middle of the month on, Venus appears as the "morning star" in the east, in the constellation Sagittarius.)

1999: Jupiter and Venus can be found low in the west after sunset. Saturn is in Pisces. (Mars, visible after midnight, moves from Virgo into Libra late in the month.)

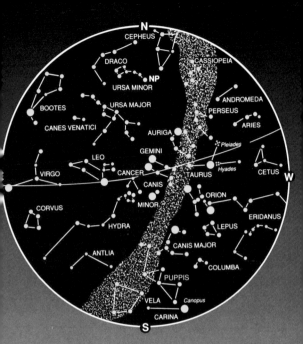

Celestial Events during March

Spring officially begins on March 20 every year from 1997 to 1999.
1997: On the 8th a total solar eclipse occurs over eastern Russia; it is
visible as a partial eclipse in China, Japan, and Southeast Asia. On the
23rd to 24th there is a partial lunar eclipse (10:00 P.M.–1:21 A.M.)
visible in the United States, Mexico, southern Europe, and northern
Africa. Mars is in Leo, on the 17th in its best viewing position of the year.
1998: From the 10th to the 30th, Mercury shows up clearly in the
evening in the western sky. (Venus appears as the "morning star" and is in
its best position in relation to the sun on the 27th.)
1999: Venus shines as the bright "evening star" in the west at sunset.
Jupiter and tiny Mercury may be glimpsed low in the west at sunset early
in the month. Venus and Saturn move from Pisces into Aries during March.
Mars, in Libra, rises at 10:30 P.M.

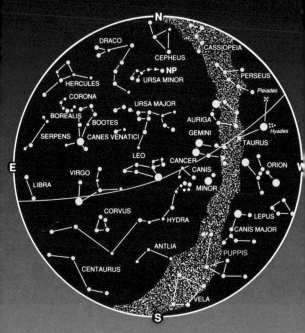

Celestial Events during April

In many countries daylight saving time is in effect at this point.

1997: During the first half of the month, Mercury appears low in the western sky after sunset. Mars is in Leo. (Jupiter is in Capricorn in the eastern sky from 4 A.M. on.)

1998: April 28 marks the beginning of the year 1419 in the Islamic calendar. There are no planets in the evening sky. (At dawn Venus and Jupiter appear close together in the eastern sky.)

1999: Venus is the bright "evening star" high in the west at sunset. Mars has made a loop back into Virgo and rises about 8:30 P.M. On the 24th, it will be in its best viewing position of the year. No other planets are visible until the end of the month when Jupiter begins to appear low in the morning twilight. (It is joined by faint Mercury which passes it May 1st.)

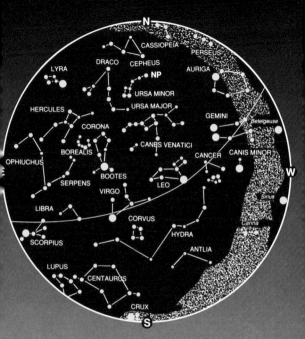

Celestial Events during May

1997: May 9 marks the beginning of the Islamic new year. Mars is in Leo. (Jupiter is in Capricorn in the eastern sky from 2 A.M. on.)

1998: There are no planets in the evening sky. (At dawn Venus and Jupiter can be seen close together in the eastern sky; at the end of the month Saturn joins them in Pisces in a rare conjunction of three planets.)

1999: Venus and Mars are both well placed for observing this month. Venus can be found high in the west shining brilliantly with an unmistakable white light. Mars in Virgo is almost equally high in the southeast and glows a bright orange color. (Shortly before sunrise Jupiter appears low in the eastern sky, with tiny Mercury near it on the 1st.)

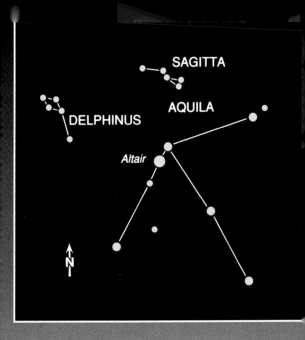

Aquila (the Eagle)

Of the constellations that do not appear in the round star maps, some of the most important ones will be individually presented here. Aquila is bordered by Delphinus (the Dolphin) on the northeast and by Sagitta (the Arrow) on the north. The four stars arranged in a diamond shape are the most striking feature of Delphinus. Sagitta is said to represent the arrow with which Hercules killed the gods' eagle. The star Altair in Aquila—along with Vega in Lyra and Deneb in Cygnus (see page 59)—is one of the brightest stars in the northern summer sky (see map NI/September on page 25). It is 16 light-years away (that amounts to 94 trillion miles or 151 trillion km) and thus one of our solar system's close neighbors.

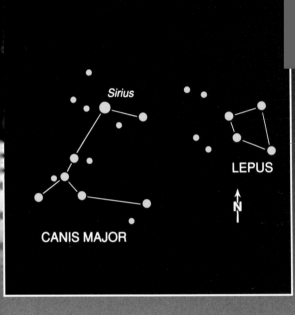

Canis Major (the Great Dog) and Lepus (the Hare)

By far the most conspicuous part of Canis Major is Sirius, the brightest star in the sky (only some of the planets outshine it). There are stars that generate a lot more light than Sirius does, but Sirius is fairly close to us: A "mere" 8.9 light-years or 53 trillion miles (85 trillion km) separate us from it. Because of this proximity a relatively large amount of light reaches Earth from this star, just as a light bulb directly overhead appears brighter to us than the much more powerful beam of a light-house that is far away. The apparent brightness of stars thus tells us something not only about their light output but also about their distance.

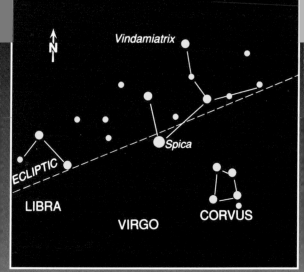

Virgo Cluster

Vindamiatrix

N

Spica

ECLIPTIC

LIBRA

VIRGO

CORVUS

Virgo (the Maiden), Corvus (the Crow or Raven), Libra (the Scales)

Of these constellations only Virgo contains components of special interest. There is first of all the star Spica, which according to Greek myth is the ear of wheat the maiden (daughter of Ceres) held in her hand. Spica (distance from Earth: 218 light-years) can be located just like Arcturus (in Boötes) by extending the curve of the Big Dipper's handle (see N 1/July on page 23). Another reason for Virgo's fame is the so-called Virgo Cluster. Here 22 percent of all the known galaxies of the northern celestial hemisphere are crowded together in a very small area. This is a truly amazing concentration of galaxies, most of which can, however, be seen only through very large telescopes. Galaxies are huge disk-shaped formations of stars, gasses, and dust that are many thousand light-years away from us.

Zodiacal Constellation 56

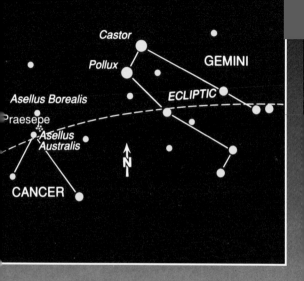

Cancer (the Crab) and Gemini (the Twins)

Praesepe, or the Beehive, is one of the best known open star clusters. At a distance of 550 light-years, about 500 stars are gathered there and present an impressive sight when viewed through binoculars. The name Praesepe (Latin for "manger") goes back to astronomers of antiquity who saw in the two stars near Praesepe two asses eating from a manger and thus named the stars Asellus Borealis and Asellus Australis. In addition to open star clusters there are globular star clusters (see the constellations Centaurus and Crux, page 76). In open clusters the stars are not as densely packed as in globular ones, which also contain many more stars than the former (up to several million).

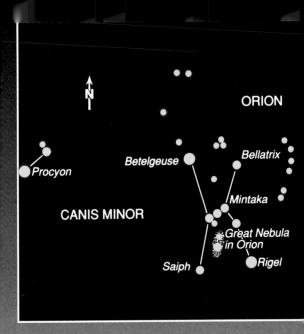

Orion and Canis Minor (the Small Dog)

Orion, which stands for the wild hunter of the same name in Greek mythology, is one of the most impressive constellations in the sky. Especially famous is the Great Nebula in Orion (M 42), a radiant gas cloud in outer space that can be seen on a clear night with the naked eye. By contrast, Canis Minor has only one brilliant star, Procyon. A comparison of the distances from Earth of some of the brightest stars is interesting. Procyon: 11 light-years; Betelgeuse: 470 light-years; Rigel: 1,300 light-years. Yet all three appear to us equidistant from Earth! Our vision is not equipped to register such mind-boggling distances spatially the way our eyes inform us that a house across the street is closer than the mountain seen in the distance behind it.

Cygnus (the Swan) and Lyra (the Lyre)

According to Greek myth, Lyra was the musical instrument the famous singer Orpheus played, and Cygnus was the swan in whose guise Zeus approached Leda. Modern astronomy has detected interesting double stars in these two constellations. Two or more stars revolving around a central point of gravity—somewhat similar to the way the planets revolve around our sun—are a rather common phenomenon in outer space. To view the star Albireo in Cygnus it is best to look through a small telescope; Epsilon Lyrae will appear double without magnification to stargazers with keen eyesight.

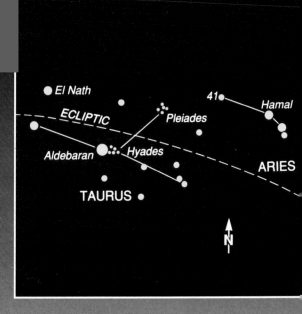

Aries (the Ram) and Taurus (the Bull)

The Pleiades and the Hyades, both in Taurus and clearly visible to the naked eye, are considered the most beautiful star clusters. The Pleiades were named by the Greeks for the seven daughters of the giant Atlas, and they are therefore also known as the Seven Sisters (distance from Earth: 450 light-years). Photographs taken through large telescopes show them in color (see front cover). In connection with the constellation Aries a note on star nomenclature may be in order. Most stars do not have proper names but are designated by a Greek letter or a number, followed by the possessive form of the constellation's Latin name. An example of this is "41 Arietis" in the map above.

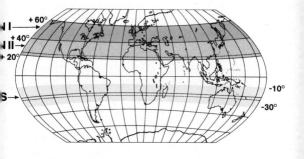

Star Maps and Constellations

The maps in Series S are for the latitudes between 10 to 30 degrees south. They are applicable for Brazil, Peru, Bolivia, South Africa, Tanzania, Botswana, Madagascar, Australia, and New Zealand.

Reminders

Before you use the maps of this series, it is important to remember this directive: When you watch the sky, the letter indicating the direction in which you face must point downward. This means that when you look northward the book will be upside down (see page 16). The familiar constellations of the northern sky then seem to be upside down compared to how we think of them, and the southern sky thus presents a somewhat unfamiliar aspect to observers from the northern half of the globe.

The initials "LMC" and "SMC" used in some of the maps that follow stand for the Large and the Small Magellanic Clouds (see pages 13, 75, and 78). The sky of the southern hemisphere includes many constellations with strange names, such as Antlia, the Air Pump. These constellations were not named until the eighteenth century (see page 11).

Celestial Events during June

In the southern hemisphere winter officially begins on June 20 in 1996, and on June 21 in 1997, and 1998.

1996: Jupiter is in Sagittarius. (From the 10th to the 30th, Mercury can be seen before sunrise in the northeast, where it is joined at 6 A.M. by Mars and Venus, which appear low above the horizon.)

1997: On the 13th the moon covers Mars. This can be observed from Africa and the Indian Ocean. Mars is in Leo and Virgo; Jupiter, in Capricorn in the east from 10 P.M. on. (From 3 A.M. on Saturn is in Pisces in the eastern sky.)

1998: There are no planets in the evening sky. (Jupiter is in the eastern sky from 2 A.M. on and Saturn from 3 A.M. on, the former in Aquarius and the latter in Aries. Venus appears in the eastern sky about two hours before sunrise.)

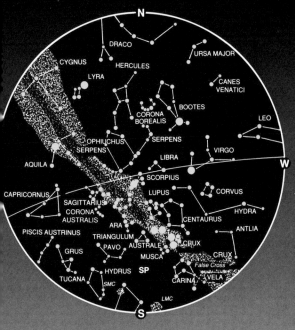

Celestial Events during July

he distance between Earth and the sun is at its annual maximum of 94.3
illion miles (152.1 million km). This occurs on July 5 in 1996 and on
e 4th in 1997 and 1998 (see Star Map N 1/January).

996: On the 4th, Jupiter is in Sagittarius in its best position in relation to
e sun. (Saturn is in Pisces in the eastern sky from 1 A.M. on. Venus can
e seen close to Mars from 4 A.M. on in the east, in the constellation
aurus.)

997: Venus shines as the "evening star" in Leo; Mars is in Virgo, and
piter, in Capricorn. (From midnight on Saturn is in Pisces in the eastern sky.)

998: In the middle of the month Mercury can be seen after sunset low in
e western sky. Jupiter is in Aquarius and Pisces in the eastern sky after
0 P.M. (Saturn is in Aries in the eastern sky from 2 A.M. on, and from
A.M. on Venus is in Taurus, also in the east.)

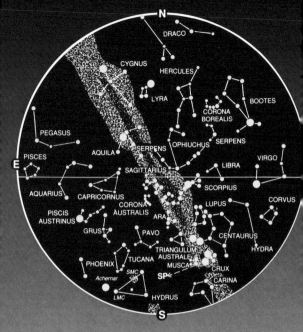

Celestial Events during August

1996: From the 10th through the 30th, Mercury can be seen low in the western sky. Jupiter is in Sagittarius; Saturn, in Pisces. (Venus shines brightly in the east before sunrise. It is in Gemini and, on the 20th, in its best position in relation to the sun.)

1997: During the first half of the month, Mercury can be seen in the western sky after sunset. On the 9th, Jupiter is in its best viewing position of the year, in Capricorn. Mars is in Virgo; Saturn, in Pisces. Venus shines brightly in Leo and Virgo.

1998: On the 21st there is an annular solar eclipse over the Pacific, visible from Australia and New Zealand as a partial eclipse. Jupiter is in Pisces; Saturn, in Aries in the eastern sky from 11 P.M. on.

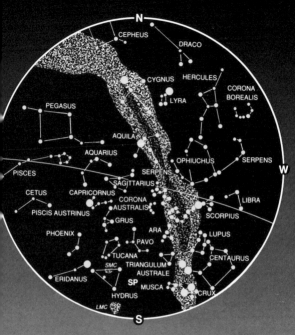

elestial Events during September

oring officially begins at the same time that fall begins in the north.

96: September 14 marks the beginning of the year 5757 according to
e Jewish calendar. On the 26th there is a total lunar eclipse that is visible
om South America, western Africa, and the Atlantic. On the 26th, Saturn
in its best viewing position of the year, in Pisces. Jupiter is in Sagittarius.
n the 4th, Venus and Mars are in Cancer from 4 A.M. on.)

97: On the 1st there is a partial solar eclipse over Australia, New
aland, and the Pacific. This is followed on the 16th by a total lunar
lipse over Australia, southern Africa, and the Indian Ocean. Venus and
ars are in Libra, Jupiter is in Capricorn, and Saturn appears in Pisces.

98: September 21 marks the beginning of the year 5759 according to
e Jewish calendar. On the 16th, Jupiter is in its best viewing position of the
ar, in Aquarius and Pisces. Saturn is in Aries from 10 P.M. on.

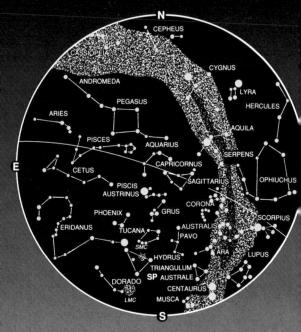

Celestial Events during October

1996: Saturn is in Pisces; Jupiter, in Sagittarius. (Mars can be seen from 5 A.M. on in the east, in the constellation Leo.)

1997: October 2 marks the beginning of the year 5758 according to the Jewish calendar. On the 10th, Saturn is in its best viewing position of the year, in Pisces. Jupiter is in Capricorn. On the 26th, Mars and Venus appear close together in Scorpius.

1998: On the 23rd, Saturn is in its best viewing position of the year, in Aries. Jupiter is in Aquarius. (From 5 A.M. on Mars is in the eastern sky, in the constellation Leo.)

Celestial Events during November

1996: Jupiter is in Sagittarius; Saturn, in Pisces. (From 3 A.M. on Mars
is in Leo in the northeast. Venus appears one hour later in the southeast,
in the constellation Virgo.)

1997: From November 20 through December 5 Mercury can be seen
low in the western sky after the sun has set. Venus is in its best position
in relation to the sun on the 6th; together with Mars it can be seen in
the west, in the constellation Sagittarius. Jupiter is in Capricorn; Saturn,
in Pisces.

1998: In the middle of the month, Mercury appears in the evening low
in the western sky. Jupiter is in Pisces; Saturn, in Aries. (From 4 A.M. on
Mars is in Leo in the eastern sky.) In the early morning hours of the 17th
the observer may see an unusually plentiful meteor shower in the
constellation Leo, the so-called Leonids.

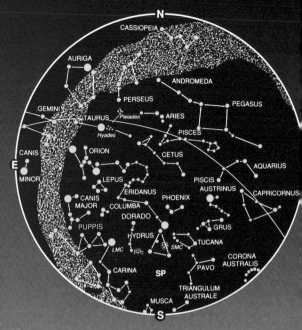

Celestial Events during December

In the southern hemisphere summer officially begins during this month. The date is December 21 for 1996 through 1999.

1996: From the 5th through the 29th, Mercury is prominent in the evening low in the western sky. Saturn is in Pisces. (From 2 A.M. on Mars is in the eastern sky, in the constellation Leo, and Venus appears shortly before sunrise.)

1997: On the 22nd, Mars and Venus move close together low in the western sky. Jupiter is in Capricorn; Saturn, in Pisces.

1998: Jupiter is in Pisces; Saturn, in Aries. (From 1 A.M. on Mars is in Virgo in the east, and during the second half of the month Mercury can be seen low over the eastern horizon shortly before sunrise.)

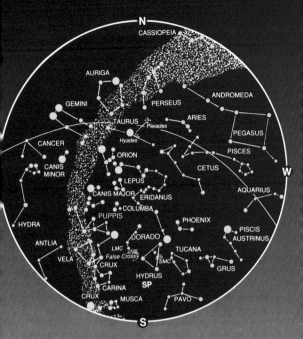

Celestial Events during January

In early January the distance between Earth and the sun reaches its annual minimum: 91.3 million miles (147.1 million km). For details, see Star Map N I/January.

1997: Saturn is in Pisces. (From midnight on, Mars is in the east in the constellation Virgo. At the end of the month Mercury appears before sunrise.)

1998: On January 5 the moon covers Saturn. This can be observed from southern Africa and from the Indian Ocean. January 28 marks the beginning of the Year of the Tiger according to the Chinese and Japanese calendar. Saturn is in Pisces, and Mars and Jupiter are very close together in Aquarius.

1999: Venus can be seen shining brightly in the early evening twilight in the west. Early in the month, Jupiter moves from Aquarius to join Saturn in Pisces. (Mars rises after midnight in the east where it can be seen for the rest of the night in Virgo.)

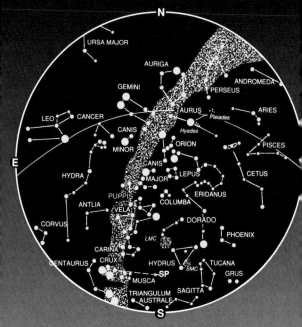

Celestial Events during February

1997: According to the Chinese and Japanese calendar, the Year of the Ox begins on February 7. Saturn is in Pisces; Mars, from 11 P.M. on, in Virgo in the eastern sky.

1998: On the 26th there is a total solar eclipse over the Pacific Ocean and over Venezuela. It is visible as a partial eclipse from all parts of South America. At dusk Mars and Venus are very close together low in the western sky. (Venus shines in the east, in the constellation Sagittarius.)

1999: On February 16, an annular eclipse of the sun, which reaches maximum at 1:34 A.M., can be seen from the Indian Ocean and western and northern Australia. This will be visible as a partial eclipse from southern Africa, the rest of Australia, Indonesia, and Antarctica. Jupiter and Venus can be found low in the west after sunset. Saturn is in Pisces. (Mars, visible after midnight, moves from Virgo into Libra late in the month.)

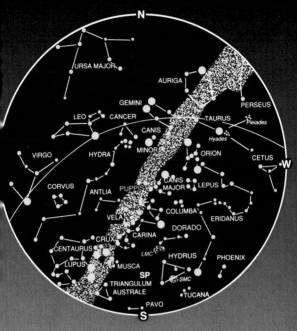

Celestial Events during March

all officially begins in the southern hemisphere at the same time spring does in the north. The date is the same for all three years: March 20. At this point the sun is positioned straight above the equator.

1997: On the 23rd to 24th there is a partial lunar eclipse (10:00 P.M. to 1:21 A.M.) over South America, southern Africa, and the southern Atlantic. On the 17th, Mars is in its best annual viewing position, in Leo. (Jupiter is in Capricorn in the southeastern sky from 3 A.M. on.)

1998: There are no planets in the evening sky.

1999: Venus shines as the bright "evening star" in the west at sunset. Saturn is above it, much fainter and a bit to the south. Both planets start the month in Pisces and move into Aries during March. Mars, in Libra rises around 10:30 P.M. Jupiter and Mercury may be glimpsed low in the west at sunset early in the month.

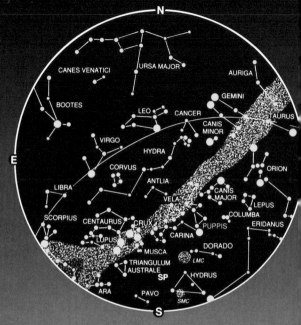

Celestial Events during April

1997: Mars is in Leo. (Jupiter can be seen from 2 A.M. on in Capricorn in the eastern sky.)

1998: April 28 marks the beginning of the year 1419 according to the Islamic calendar. There are no planets in the evening sky. (From 4 A.M. on Venus and Jupiter can be seen close together in the east, in the constellation Aquarius.)

1999: Venus is the bright "evening star" high in the west at sunset. Mars has made a loop back into Virgo and rises about 8:30 P.M. On the 24th, it will be in its best viewing position of the year. No other planets are visible until the end of the month when Jupiter begins to appear low in the morning twilight.

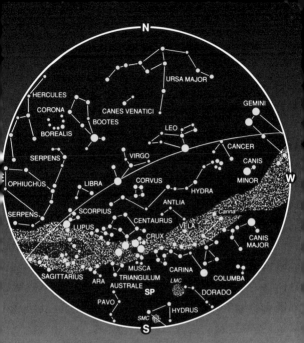

Celestial Events during May

1997: May 9 marks the beginning of the year 1418 according to the Islamic calendar. Mars is in Leo. (Jupiter is in Capricorn in the eastern sky from 1 A.M. on, and in the second half of the month Mercury can be seen low in the east shortly before sunrise.)

1998: There are no planets in the evening sky. (Venus and Jupiter appear close together in the eastern sky at dawn. At the end of the month Saturn joins them; and, since Mercury also appears early in May, the stargazer has a chance to observe the spectacular sight of four planets in close proximity to each other.)

1999: Venus can be found high in the west shining brilliantly with an unmistakable white light. Mars in Virgo is almost equally high in the southeast and glows a bright orange color. (Shortly before sunrise Jupiter appears low in the eastern sky.)

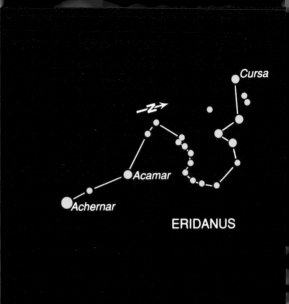

Eridanus

You may notice that in this picture the arrow pointing north is in an almost horizontal position rather than in a more or less vertical one. We had to draw Eridanus in this position because otherwise it would not have fit the format of the illustrations. Eridanus is one of the longest constellations in the sky, extending from Orion almost to the south pole (indicated in star maps by the letters SP). Eridanus has one star that deserves special mention: Achernar, one of the brightest stars in the southern celestial hemisphere. It is 78 light-years distant from Earth. In Greek mythology Eridanus is a river that figures in many stories, and the stars that make up this constellation form a curvy line across the sky that resembles a meandering river.

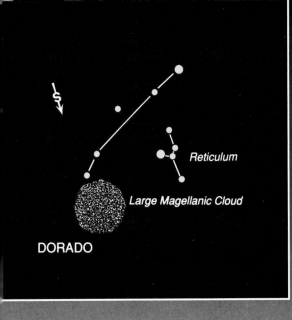

Reticulum

Large Magellanic Cloud

DORADO

Dorado

The constellation Dorado was first identified by the German astronomer Johann Bayer in 1603. Within its confines there is a truly "golden" heavenly object: the Large Magellanic Cloud (see color photo on page 13). It is today a major focus of scientific research conducted at observatories located in the southern hemisphere. Because it is so close to Earth, it appears as the brightest and most impressive galaxy outside of the Milky Way. It is composed of 18 to 20 billion stars and is removed from us by about 150,000 light-years. The Large Magellanic Cloud is clearly visible to the unaided eye—even at full moon!

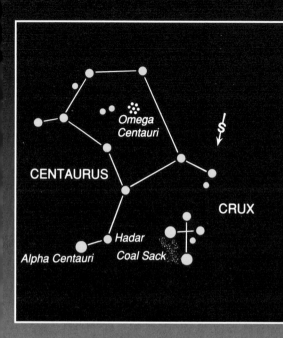

Crux (the Southern Cross) and Centaurus

Here we are contemplating one of the most beautiful, star-studded regions of the sky. The famous Southern Cross (Crux) was used as a guide by sailors of earlier ages to establish the points of the compass on the high sea, for the central axis of the cross points toward the south celestial pole (SP) (see maps S/February and S/August on pages 70 and 64). The Coalsack, one of the darkest spots in the beautiful, luminous band of the Milky Way, is located in the area of the Southern Cross. Here, dense dust clouds, acting like a wall, block the view to the stars beyond them. Toliman in the constellation Centaurus, also known as Alpha Centauri, is the closest star to Earth—4.2 light-years or 25 trillion miles (40 trillion km) away. Omega Centauri is the brightest globular star cluster in the sky.

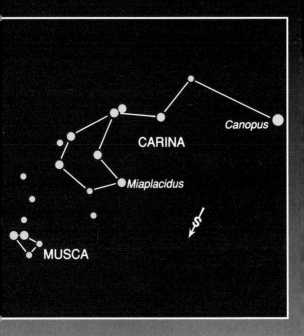

Carina (the Keel) and Musca (the Fly)

One of the most exciting stories of Greek mythology tells about the ship Argos and the heroic feats accomplished by its crew, the Argonauts. No wonder the gods elevated this legendary ship to the heavens. It took up a large area below Canis Major and Orion—indeed, too large an area according to modern astronomy, which regards constellations as nothing more than a useful device for subdividing the sky. Argo Navis has therefore been cut up into three sections: Puppis (the Poop), Vela (the Sail), and Carina. Carina contains Canopus, the second brightest star in the sky. A star of superlatives, Canopus shines 20,000 times more brightly than the sun and is 60 times its size. Its distance from Earth is 370 light-years.

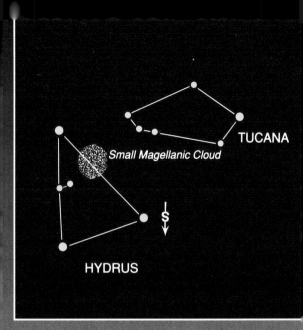

Hydrus (the Small Water Snake) and Tucana (the Toucan)

The sky of the southern hemisphere is especially rich in exotic names for constellations. One example is Tucana, which is the name of a South American bird family. Hydrus, which is next to Tucana, contains one of the most interesting objects of the southern sky, namely, the Small Magellanic Cloud. This cloud was discovered by Ferdinand Magellan, who was the first to circumnavigate the world in the years 1519 to 1522. The Small and the Large Magellanic Clouds (see Constellation Dorado on page 75 and the color photo on page 13) are our closest galactic neighbors, being "a mere" 150,000 light-years away from us. There, many million stars combine in formations that are similar to our Milky Way Galaxy. The Small Magellanic Cloud can be seen only from the southern hemisphere, but from there it is visible to the naked eye.

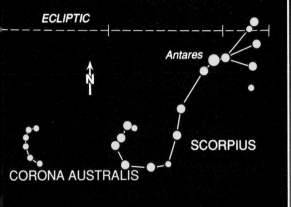

Scorpius (the Scorpion) and Corona Australis (the Southern Crown)

The twelve constellations of the zodiac, such as Scorpius, Aries, and Sagittarius, all lie along the ecliptic. To be quite exact, the ecliptic transects thirteen constellations, the thirteenth being Ophiuchus (the Serpent Bearer). The above diagram depicts the exact course of the ecliptic in that section of the sky and also shows that Scorpius was assigned only a tiny section of the ecliptic. You look in vain for Ophiuchus (the Serpent Bearer) among the signs of the zodiac listed in horoscopes. This is one more clear indication that the signs of the zodiac are not identical with the zodiacal constellations.

The reddish star Antares is a true giant. It is 740 times the size of our sun!

Table of Lunar Phases

	Jan	Feb	Mar	Apr	May	Jun	Jul	Aug	Sep	Oct	Nov	Dec
1996	5 ○	4 ○	5 ○	3 ○	3 ○	1 ○	7 ●	6 ●	4 ●	4 ●	3 ●	3 ●
	13 ◑	12 ◑	12 ◑	10 ●	9 ●	8 ●	15 ○	14 ○	12 ●	**12** ●	10 ◑	10 ◑
	20 ●	19 ●	19 ●	**17** ◑	17 ◑	15 ◑	23 ◑	21 ◑	20 ○	19 ○	17 ○	17 ○
	27 ◑	26 ◑	26 ◑	25 ○	25 ○	24 ○	30 ○	28 ○	**26** ○	26 ◑	24 ◑	24 ◑
						30 ○						
1997	1 ●	7 ●	2 ●	7 ●	6 ●	5 ●	4 ●	3 ●	1 ●	1 ●	7 ○	7 ○
	8 ◑	14 ◑	**8** ◑	14 ◑	14 ◑	12 ○	12 ○	11 ○	9 ○	9 ○	14 ◑	13 ◑
	15 ○	22 ○	15 ○	22 ○	22 ○	20 ◑	19 ◑	18 ◑	**16** ◑	15 ◑	21 ●	21 ●
	23 ◑		**23** ◑	29 ●	29 ●	27 ●	26 ●	24 ●	23 ●	22 ●	29 ●	29 ●
	31 ●		31 ●							31 ●		
1998	5 ●	3 ●	5 ●	3 ●	3 ●	1 ●	1 ●	7 ○	6 ○	5 ○	4 ○	3 ○
	12 ◑	11 ◑	12 ◑	11 ◑	11 ◑	10 ○	9 ○	14 ◑	12 ◑	12 ◑	10 ◑	10 ◑
	20 ○	19 ○	21 ○	19 ○	18 ○	17 ◑	16 ◑	**21** ●	20 ●	20 ●	18 ●	18 ●
	28 ◑	**26** ◑	28 ◑	26 ●	25 ●	23 ●	23 ●	30 ●	28 ●	28 ●	26 ●	26 ●
							31 ●					
1999	1 ○	8 ●	2 ○	8 ●	8 ●	7 ●	6 ●	4 ●	2 ●	2 ●	7 ○	7 ○
	9 ◑	**16** ◑	10 ◑	15 ◑	15 ◑	13 ○	12 ○	**11** ○	9 ○	9 ○	16 ◑	15 ◑
	17 ○	22 ○	17 ○	22 ○	22 ○	20 ◑	20 ◑	18 ◑	17 ◑	17 ◑	23 ●	22 ●
	24 ●		24 ●	30 ●	30 ●	28 ●	**28** ●	26 ●	25 ●	24 ●	29 ●	29 ●
	31 ●		31 ○							31 ●		

● = New moon   ◑ = First quarter   ○ = Full moon   ◐ = Last quarter

A number in boldface type with ● = Solar eclipse; with ○ = lunar eclipse